Tech 2.0

World-Changing Social Media Companies

Facebook®

by John Csiszar

Tech 2.0

World-Changing Social Media Companies

Facebook®

Instagram®

Reddit®

Snapchat®

Twitter®

WhatsApp®

Tech 2.0

World-Changing Social Media Companies

Facebook®

by John Csiszar

Mason Crest

Mason Crest
450 Parkway Drive, Suite D
Broomall, PA 19008
www.masoncrest.com

© 2019 by Mason Crest, an imprint of National Highlights, Inc.

Printed and bound in the United States of America.

Series ISBN: 978-1-4222-4060-1
Hardback ISBN: 978-1-4222-4061-8
EBook ISBN: 978-1-4222-7728-7

First printing
1 3 5 7 9 8 6 4 2

Produced by Shoreline Publishing Group LLC
Santa Barbara, California
Editorial Director: James Buckley Jr.
Designer: Patty Kelley
www.shorelinepublishing.com
Cover photograph by Pressureua/Dreamstime.com

Library of Congress Cataloging-in-Publication Data
Names: Csiszar, John, author. Title: Facebook / by John Csiszar. Description: Broomall, PA : Mason Crest, [2018] | Series: Tech 2.0: world-changing social media companies | Includes index.
Identifiers: LCCN 2017053411| ISBN 9781422240618 (hardback) | ISBN 9781422240601 (series) | ISBN 9781422277287 (ebook)
Subjects: LCSH: Facebook (Electronic resource)--Juvenile literature. | Facebook (Firm)--Juvenile literature. | Online social networks--History--Juvenile literature.
Classification: LCC HM743.F33 C795 2018 | DDC 302.30285--dc23 LC record available at https://lccn.loc.gov/2017053411

QR Codes disclaimer:

CONTENTS

KEY ICONS TO LOOK FOR

Words to Understand: These words with their easy-to-understand definitions will increase the reader's understanding of the text, while building vocabulary skills.

Sidebars: This boxed material within the main text allows readers to build knowledge, gain insights, explore possibilities, and broaden their perspectives by weaving together additional information to provide realistic and holistic perspectives.

Educational Videos: Readers can view videos by scanning our QR codes, providing them with additional educational content to supplement the text. Examples include news coverage, moments in history, speeches, iconic moments, and much more!

Text-Dependent Questions: These questions send the reader back to the text for more careful attention to the evidence presented here.

Research Projects: Readers are pointed toward areas of further inquiry connected to each chapter. Suggestions are provided for projects that encourage deeper research and analysis.

Series Glossary of Key Terms: This back-of-the-book glossary contains terminology used throughout this series. Words found here increase the reader's ability to read and comprehend higher-level books and articles in this field.

Introduction

Facebook. Think about how much that single word means to many people's everyday life. If you're not one of the more than *two billion* monthly active users on Facebook—representing more than 25 percent of the world's population—it's still hard to avoid Facebook's reach. If you read news articles online, you'll likely see a link asking you to share the article on Facebook; if you walk into a store, you may see a sign asking you to "like us on Facebook."

The fact that Facebook is everywhere is a testament to its success in the field of social media. "Social media" is a way that people can connect to one another over the internet. Facebook owes its entire existence to this human need to connect, and it has found countless ways to help fulfill that desire.

Facebook famously started out in a Harvard dorm room, the brainchild of whiz kid Mark Zuckerberg. Enlisting the help of some of his friends—and later, thousands of the best engineers and computer scientists in the world—Mark found a way to tap into the basic human need for connecting to and with each other.

The result has been nothing short of astounding. Facebook, the company, was worth nearly $500 billion as of December 2017. This ranks it the fourth most-valuable company in America, behind only Apple, Alphabet (formerly Google), and Microsoft. Facebook has only existed since 2004, yet its value has already grown past well-known companies that have been in business for more than a century, such as General Electric, Johnson & Johnson, ExxonMobil, and JP Morgan Chase.

Facebook is now used by billions of people around the world. It has become one of the most successful websites on the internet today. The site has changed the way people view and use the internet, transforming the web to something personal. No matter who you are, you can have a page on Facebook that allows you to speak your mind, share photos of yourself and your friends, and tell others what you're reading or watching online. What was once a passive experience for Internet users is now something in which each person can participate.

In a recent survey, almost 25 percent of the time that people used the internet was on social networking sites like Facebook. Considering that email accounted for only about 8 percent of online time, that's a lot of time on Facebook and other sites like it! Facebook was also the site that, on average, people spent the most time on per month. On average, internet users spent around two hours per month on Google.com and Yahoo.com, around half an hour on Amazon.com, but more than *seven hours* per month on Facebook.com.

Smartphones have given people even more opportunities to access Facebook. It's the third-most popular app after email and the web browser. One survey found that 79 percent of smartphone users check their phone within fifteen minutes of waking up. Facebook accounts for about a fifth of the time users spend communicating on their smartphones, which is just slightly less than texting.

Facebook founder Mark Zuckerberg has changed the way we connect.

Going forward, the future for Facebook looks promising. Mark Zuckerberg's company has been been buying other companies, constantly looking to expand its reach and abilities. Instagram and WhatsApp, powerful companies on their own, are now working under the Facebook banner. Technologies like the Oculus virtual reality platform promise to bring science fiction into reality.

The story behind Facebook is just as exciting as the technologies it has unleashed onto the world. From humble beginnings to rapid growth, the company has hit a few bumps along the way, some of which have (and continue to be) controversial. However, with Mark Zuckerberg's vision leading the way, Facebook has continued onward and upward to become a true giant of technology.

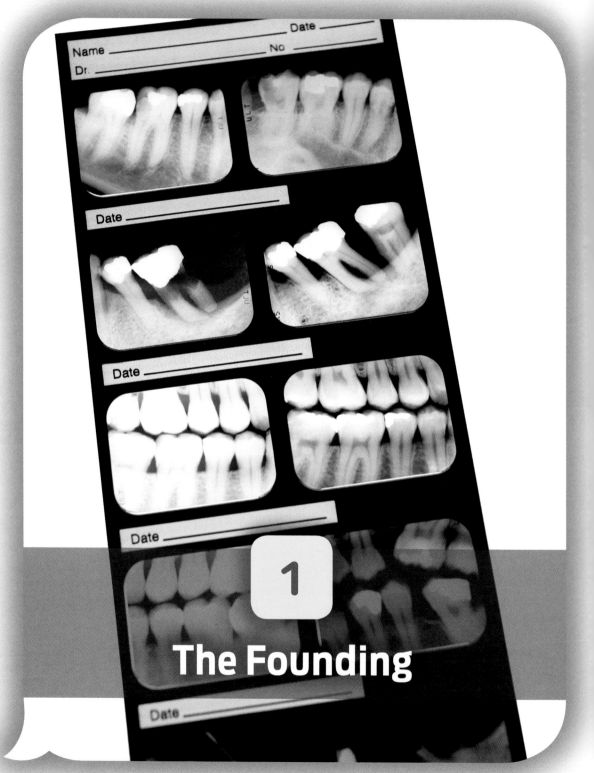

The Founding

As seen in the movie *The Social Network*, Facebook was primarily the **brainchild** of Harvard University student Mark Zuckerberg. While he would later develop the idea with his friends Eduardo Saverin, Chris Hughes, and Dustin Moskovitz, Mark developed a few ideas that became Facebook on his own.

How did Mark get on the path to such game-changing tech to start with? He actually started at an early age, thanks to the technology in his father Edward's dental office.

Edward's dental practice featured early computer technology, particularly when it came to X-rays and organizing the office. That experience with technology rubbed off on his son Mark, helping to shape his interests early in his life. Edward introduced Mark to computer programming. He showed his son how to program using an Atari computer, an early, simple kind of home computer, much less powerful than the computers

WORDS TO UNDERSTAND

boarding school a type of high school at which students live full-time during the school year

brainchild an invention

incorporate sold shares of stock to become a publicly traded company

in our homes today. Mark learned quickly, and he soon found he loved computers and programming.

In 1996, Edward was looking for a way for his receptionist to tell him that a patient had arrived in the waiting room. Up to that point, his receptionist had simply been yelling into the office, and Edward wanted something more efficient. Twelve-year-old Mark saw that a computer program could help solve his father's problem. He set to work to create software that could help.

The program that Mark built let the computers in his father's office and in the Zuckerberg house send messages back

This is the humble high school that Mark quickly outgrew.

and forth. Mark called his creation Zucknet. The program's name was a reference to Mark's nickname, "Zuck."

A year later, America Online (AOL) released its own messaging program, called Instant Messenger. Mark had already seen the potential for computers to communicate with each other over the Internet. Zucknet allowed Edward's receptionist to send a message to him whenever a patient arrived. Using the program Mark created, Edward and his family could send messages between the computers in their home, as well. One night, Mark used Zucknet to send a gag message to his sister Donna while she did her homework. The message said that a computer virus would cause the computer she was on to explode in thirty seconds!

New School, New Ideas

Mark started at Ardsley High School, located in Ardsley, New York. There, Mark studied hard and got excellent grades. He was particularly interested in Greek and Latin studies. Mark loved to read classical literature, and he enjoyed taking classes on the languages in which works like *The Iliad* and *The Odyssey* were originally written. By Mark's sophomore year, his family realized he needed more than what Ardsley High School could offer him. Mark moved to a **boarding school** called Phillips Exeter Academy (Exeter for short), located in New Hampshire.

At Exeter, Mark continued to do very well, both in school and in activities outside the classroom. He kept up his love of classical literature, Latin, and Greek. Mark also became an excellent fencer and became captain of Exeter's fencing team by the time he graduated from the school. In addition, he won prizes for his work in math, physics, and astronomy, as well as for his studies in Latin and Greek.

Though he was always able to succeed in the classroom, Mark's passion for computers never took a back seat to his other activities. While at Exeter, he continued to learn more about computer programming and creating new software.

During his senior year, Mark created a computer program for his senior project called Synapse Media Player. Synapse was a program that recorded what kind of music users liked to hear, keeping track of the songs and artists they enjoyed. The program then automatically picked new artists, new songs, and new playlists for users based on the music they'd already picked. The website called Pandora.com picks music for users in a similar way, based on what they already like. At the time, however, Mark's Synapse Media Player was a brand-new idea. What started as a senior project from a high school student quickly spread on the Internet. Blogs and websites wrote about Synapse, and Internet users began downloading the project for themselves. To put Synapse into the world, Mark started a company he called Intelligent Media Group.

Big technology companies started to take notice of Mark's program and the buzz that it was getting on the Internet. Soon, Microsoft and AOL were both trying to buy Synapse from Mark

At Philips Exeter in New Hampshire, Mark created his first computer programs.

and offering him jobs creating software at their companies. Mark turned them both down and decided instead to go on to college after graduating from Exeter. Mark wasn't even eighteen yet, but he already showed great promise.

On to Harvard

The early ideas for Facebook came about during Mark's second year at Harvard. Mark created a program called Course-Match, which allowed users to decide on which classes to take based on other people in the class. He also created a website called Facemash, a very simple site that allowed users to see photos of two people and then vote on who was better looking. The site used photos of students at Harvard, which Mark got by hacking Harvard's computer network. In its first few hours on-line, a few hundred people visited Facemash.

Over the next few days, the site was shared with people around Harvard, leading the school's administration to take no-

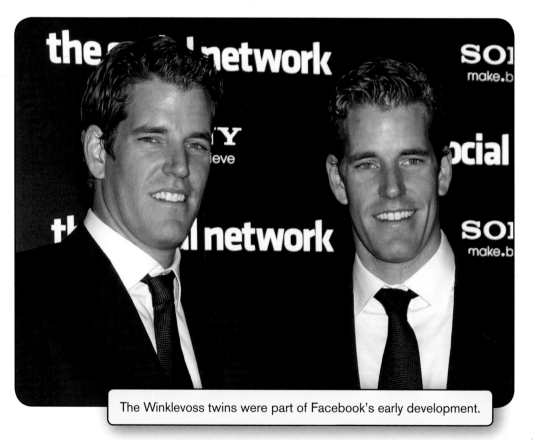

The Winklevoss twins were part of Facebook's early development.

tice and shut down the site. The administration was furious that Mark had gotten through the security surrounding their network. They threatened to kick him out of school, but eventually, they decided to let him stay.

After Facemash was shut down, articles about Mark appeared in the Harvard student newspaper, and students were both outraged and interested in their fellow classmate. Soon, three students looking to start their own site came to Mark for help. Divya Narendra and Cameron and Tyler Winklevoss wanted to create a website that allowed students at Harvard to find each other online, share information, and possibly begin dating. They called the site Harvard Connection. Mark agreed to help Narendra and the Winklevoss brothers (two twins who were known to other students for their spots on Harvard's rowing team) in the creation of Harvard Connection.

Mark worked with Narendra and the Winklevoss twins on Harvard Connection, but it wasn't long before he stopped working on the site. Instead, he began work on his own web project, a site that allowed users to post information about themselves and see information posted by other students. He called his site TheFacebook.com, based, many believe, on the books Exeter gave students that included pictures, addresses, and phone numbers for every student in the school. "Face books" were a way for students to get to know each other at a new school, and Mark thought a similar idea could work online. Mark wanted the site to be easy to use and reasonably simple, so that anyone could use it. He made the main color on the site blue, because of his color-blindness; he can't see red or green. Blue was the color Mark could see most clearly, making the decision to go with blue and white an easy one. "Blue is the richest color for me," he later told an interviewer. "I can see all of blue."

TheFacebook.com

In his sophomore year at Harvard, Mark launched TheFacebook.com as a way for students at the university to share information. The reaction from students on campus was very positive, and the site became quite popular. Students began sharing information about themselves, creating profiles and pages that explained their interests and contained their photos. Within one month of the site's launch on February 4, 2004, almost half of Harvard undergraduate students had signed up for TheFacebook.com and created their own pages on the site.

Here is a screen grab of one of the pages of TheFacebook.

After the successful launch of TheFacebook.com, Mark turned to his friends at Harvard, Eduardo Saverin, Chris Hughes, and Dustin Moskovitz, for

The Controversy Over Facebook's Founding

Despite the early success of Mark's Facebook.com, the site's beginnings were controversial. The students who worked with Mark for a little while on Harvard Connection believe that Mark stole the idea for Facebook from them. "[Mark] stole the moment, he stole the idea, and he stole the execution," Cameron Winklevoss told an interviewer years later. A few days after Mark launched The-Facebook.com at Harvard, Divya Narendra and the Winklevoss twins, Cameron and Tyler, told the student newspaper that Mark had told them he was helping to build Harvard Connection while working on his own site based on the same idea.

They said Mark had lied to them about working on Harvard Connection and ended up taking their idea, leaving them with nothing.

Mark sees things very differently. He says that Harvard Connection focused on dating, while his site was based around the idea of sharing information. Mark has said that he created Facebook without input from the Harvard Connection project, despite the close timing of his working on Harvard Connection and starting Facebook.

Regardless of how Mark got the idea for TheFacebook.com, when the site launched, it quickly became a huge success. Though it started small, its reach grew quickly, and soon college students from all over the country were creating Facebook pages for themselves. With Mark leaving college, he'd have the time to focus on growing the site even more and creating what would become one of the Internet's biggest success stories.

more ideas about the site. The friends had long talked about how the Internet would become more and more popular, until everyone used it. Looking back on his creating TheFacebook.com, Mark told an interviewer about his discussions with his friends:

[We] would hang out and go together to Pinocchio's, the local pizza place, and talk about trends in technology. We'd say, "Isn't it obvious that everyone was going to be on the Internet? Isn't it, like, inevitable that there would be a huge social network of people?" It was something that we expected to happen. The thing that's been really surprising about the evolution of Facebook is—I think then and I think now—that if we didn't do this someone else would have done it.

Though the site began as Harvard only, Facebook soon expanded to other top-level universities, particularly with the help of Mark's friends Dustin Moskovitz and Chris Hughes. Students from Boston University, New York University, Columbia, Yale, Dartmouth, and Stanford created their own profiles. Soon, the site became open to students from colleges all over United States.

By the end of his second year at Harvard, Mark was ready to drop out of college and run Facebook full time. Soon, the compa-

Dustin Moskovitz was another early Facebook developer.

ny would become one of the internet's most successful, its website used by millions all over the world. But the company had a lot more growing to do before it would become successful.

After the launch of Facebook in early 2004, Mark left college to focus on building the site and creating a company to help manage it. He was certain he didn't need a college education to achieve his goals.

California, Here We Come

To grow the new company, Mark moved to California, met investors, and opened up Facebook to new users. Over the next few years, Facebook would become one of the most important new Internet companies in the world, and the site's popularity would grow each year. New ideas and new users kept Facebook fresh and interesting, attracting even more people to the top social networking site.

Interview with Mark Zuckerberg

Before the success, however, the company's first year began in a small house in California. With TheFacebook.com growing in popularity, Facebook **incorporated**. Sean Parker, the creator of the Internet music sharing program Napster, had been giving advice to Mark about how to grow Facebook and start a company. When Facebook officially became a company, Sean became its president.

In June of the same year, Mark moved to Palo Alto, California, with a few of the friends who'd helped him start TheFacebook.com, including Dustin Moskovitz. The group rented a small house that served as the Facebook offices, as well as the home for the people who worked at the small company.

Sean Parker advised Mark early on. He had made it big with his Napster music-sharing app.

To start a new company is very difficult. Without money to pay for things like offices, computers, and salaries, it's nearly impossible. To keep Facebook going, Mark needed to find an investor who was willing to provide the company with money to run the business. In the summer that Facebook moved to California, Mark, Dustin Moskovitz, and Chris Hughes met with a businessman named Peter Thiel.

The young face of the Internet future.

Peter is best known for having created Pay-Pal, a system that allows Internet users to pay for the things they buy online using a credit card. PayPal had become a success with the increase in the number of Internet users shopping online, and Peter had started working to find companies in which to invest. Facebook was just the right kind of company for Peter's investment. At the meeting with Mark, Dustin, and Chris, Peter agreed to give half a billion dollars to the new company.

Now Facebook had the money it needed to continue to grow, and its founders were ready to work hard to make that happen. Mark and his friends had big plans for Facebook. Moving to California was just the beginning.

Text-Dependent Questions

1. Explain how Edward Zuckerberg's profession influenced his son Mark to start creating computer programs.

2. What controversy surrounded the founding of Facebook?

3. What was Synapse Media Player?

Research Project

Choose another Internet startup story—perhaps from one of the other books in the Tech 2.0 series—and compare how its origins differed from, or were similar to, Facebook. How much did they depend on a single entrepreneur? What was the role of early investors in this other startup?

2

Facebook Takes Over

n 2005, Facebook changed the name of their site, dropping "The" from the beginning of the name. In the same year, Facebook opened its site to high school students who wanted to sign up and create their own pages. (Before that, Facebook had only been open to college students.) Then, the company allowed the employees of a few important technology companies like Apple and Microsoft to join the site and begin sharing information about themselves. About a year later, in September of 2006, Facebook opened the site to anyone older than thirteen who had an email address. From there, the company began to grow rapidly, soon reaching over 9 million users and attracting a $1 billion buyout offer from search engine giant Yahoo, which the company turned down.

Soon after, Facebook learned what many rapidly growing companies already knew—**innovation** alone is not enough to transform a company into a global powerhouse, no matter how smart the founders are. While the company may have turned down the huge cash offer from Yahoo, their patience paid off just a year later. Facebook got a massive pile of cash from one of the "old line"

WORDS TO UNDERSTAND

innovation creativity, the process of building something new

resignation the process of leaving a job or position by choice

traits particular qualities or characteristics, in this case of a person

tech companies, Microsoft. Bill Gates's huge software company invested $240 million into Facebook in October of 2007 for just a 1.6 percent stake in the company. The investment valued Facebook at $15 billion, far above the $1 billion Yahoo had offered. With this new cash, Facebook was off to the races in terms of upward growth.

By August of 2008, Facebook.com had 100 million users. Mark took note of the achievement in a blog post on the site:

Already a success, Bill Gates and Microsoft helped Facebook grow.

"We hit a big milestone today—100 million people around the world are now using Facebook. This is a really gratifying moment for us because it means a lot that you have decided that Facebook is a good, trusted place for you to share your lives with your friends. So we just wanted to take this moment to say, "thanks."

We spend all our time here trying to build the best possible product that enables you to share and stay connected, so the fact that we're growing so quickly all over the world is very rewarding. Thanks for all your support and stay tuned for more great things in the future."

Growth = $

One hundred million users might seem like a lot but that was just the start of Facebook's extraordinary growth. Only six months later, Mark posted on Facebook.com again, announcing that the site had reached 200 million people using the site. By early 2010, 400 million people had signed up for the site to share

Facebook Sparks a Revolution

On June 8, 2010, the online social network known as Facebook did something far more important than connect "friends." It sparked a revolution.

That was the day when Wael Ghonim, a twenty-nine-year-old Google marketing executive, came across an image on Facebook that made him angry. The photograph showed a young man named Khaled Mohamed Said, who had been beaten to death by the Egyptian police. Wael knew he had to take action. So he created a Facebook page. On it he wrote, "Today they killed Khaled. If I don't act for his sake, tomorrow they will kill me." He named the Facebook page "We Are All Khaled Said."

Two minutes after his Facebook page went live, three hundred people had joined it. That number climbed to a quarter million in three months. And then the voices on the Facebook page spilled out into Egypt's streets. Wael's Facebook page helped ignite the uprising that eventually led to the **resignation** of Egypt's president. It became a powerful part of the movement that's come to be known as the Arab Spring. Wael's willingness to speak out proved that one person can start a change that spreads like wildfire. But he couldn't have done it without Facebook.

"When you give everyone a voice," says Mark Zuckerberg, the founder of Facebook, "and give people power, the system usually ends up in a really good place. So, what we view our role as, is giving people that power."

That's what Mark has done through Facebook. He's given people all around the world a place to have a voice. And by doing that, he's helped to change the world in unexpected ways.

information and connect with their friends. A few months after that, in the summer of 2010, Facebook.com had half a billion people using the site.

Along with new users came more profits for Facebook. In 2006, the company made just over $50 million, a lot for a new company, but very little compared to how much Facebook would go on to make. In 2007, the company made three times what it did the year before. By 2009, Facebook made three quarters of a billion dollars, and just one year later, the company brought in around $2 billion. Facebook wasn't nearly done growing, however. Year after year, Facebook's revenue rose dramatically, topping an astounding $26.8 billion by 2016.

In just a few years, Facebook went from its beginnings in a college dorm room to becoming one of the biggest companies on the Internet. Mark's dream of creating a social networking site that allowed people from all over the world to share information about themselves with their friends and family had come true. He'd once made games and small programs in his parents' house. As of 2017, he's now running the fourth-most valu-

The rise of mobile devices was a huge boon to Facebook's growth.

At first, Facebook attracted mostly young people; its demographics have aged.

able company in America, one that many consider to be one of the most important of the internet age.

Facebook Pros and Cons

Although Facebook had become one of the most successful internet companies, many questioned whether its impact has been positive or negative. Some wonder whether Facebook. com had changed the way people communicate with each other in a way that makes relationships less meaningful.

Mark was asked whether he sees Facebook as changing the definition of friendship for a new generation, making relationships between friends less meaningful. He replied that he believes Facebook has helped people become closer, no matter how far they may be from each other geographically. "[Facebook has] always had the goal of helping people connect with all the people that they want," Mark told *Time* magazine. Mark continued:

> *Our mission hasn't been to make it so people connect with people that they didn't know. . . . It's just all about, you know, maybe you're not in the same place as your family or your friends right now, but you want to stay connected. I think Facebook gives people a tool to do that better, in ways they couldn't before. . . . What I think Facebook allows is for people to stay connected who aren't seeing each other in person everyday. . . . I don't think Facebook is taking away from any of the other interactions that you have, it's just expanding your social sphere so that you can keep in touch with all of these people. Before, you just wouldn't have had any way to do that. That makes people's lives just a bit richer.*

Others question Facebook's treatment of the privacy of its users. While Facebook is useful for sharing information, it also collects information. According to some experts, Facebook is essentially constantly watching you. Whenever you click "like," Facebook adds to its in-house profile about you. Over time, everything you post, everything you watch, everything you like online paints a picture about who you are—what you're interested in, what you respond to, even down to your specific personality **traits**.

Sports
MOVIES
Music
Animals
Books
Websites

Facebook learns what you "like" and makes sure you get more.

In an era when hacking seems commonplace, the fear is that such a vast amount of information can be used against you. For example, if you post something even marginally offensive or inappropriate, that image or statement can be recorded forever and turned up in a simple Google search. That is something that every employer, family member, or

Facebook faced early challenges to make sure its site was secure.

future spouse can find out about you for the rest of your life.

When discussing privacy with *Time* magazine, Mark said that he understands that people's privacy online is very important to them. He believes in users' ability to control what information is shared and with whom it's shared, but he also thinks that sharing photos or information about yourself with friends and family can be rewarding and important to bonding with others online. Mark has said that openly sharing information is an important part of Facebook's mission, that making the world a more open

A Visit From the President

In 2011, Mark Zuckerberg had a very special guest visit the Facebook offices. For the occasion, Mark took off his usual hooded sweatshirt and put on a suit.

When his guest saw what Mark was wearing, he grinned. "My name is Barack Obama," the visitor said, "and I'm the guy who got Mark to wear a jacket and tie. I'm very proud of that."

Not every company gets a visit from the President of the United States, but Facebook is no ordinary company. The company's website has changed the way people communicate, how people use the Internet, and the way people share information about themselves online. Mark and his company Facebook have been a leading force in the movement toward a more connected world.

President Obama noted that Facebook was part of this global change as he explained why he had decided to hold an event at the company's headquarters. "The reason we want to do this is because more and more people are getting their information through different media. Historically, part of what makes for a healthy democracy, what makes good politics, is citizens who are informed and engaged. And Facebook allows us to make sure this isn't a one-way conversation."

Facebook had made Mark the youngest billionaire in the world—and it had done a lot for the world as well.

and less secretive place is part of a change that the Internet—and social networking companies like Facebook—are helping to bring about.

Critics, however, argue that Facebook doesn't allow users enough control over their privacy. They maintain that Facebook. com doesn't give users the options they would need to keep some information from being shared with big companies looking to advertise their products to Facebook's users. These critics also say that Facebook's privacy options are too difficult to use or understand, and that these options change too often for the average person to keep up with them.

Zuckerberg and President Obama

Facebook continues to address security and safe content issues.

Facebook also has had to address challenges from goverment officials who wanted the company's help. Facebook joined with many other Internet companies in resisting early attempts to address, for example, human trafficking. Government officals wanted the companies to more carefully police and/or restrict content that could be used by such criminals. After at first resisting out of liability concerns, by late 2017, the companies had decided to do what they could to help.

Though Facebook may have its critics, and debates over privacy and online relationships will continue, there's no questioning the massive change that Facebook and other social networking sites like it have helped bring to the world.

Text-Dependent Questions

1. Describe the role Facebook played in Egyptian politics back in 2010.

2. What key role did Microsoft play in the growth of Facebook?

3. How does founder Mark Zuckerberg respond to concerns over Facebook's privacy issues?

4. How has Facebook changed the nature of communication in personal relationships?

Research Project

This chapter discusses how Facebook was used to inspire a revolution in Egypt. Using newspapers, magazines, or the Internet, find a recent news story that shows Facebook and its role in American politics. Describe how Facebook was used in this instance to influence people's opinions.

3

Game-Changing Tech

Although the movie *The Social Network* (left) may suggest that Facebook was the first and last social network, that's not the case. Other companies, such as Friendster and MySpace, got to the social network audience long before Facebook did. So why did Facebook come to be considered *the* social network? The answer is a combination of factors. For one, as we've already seen, Facebook chief Mark Zuckerberg is a unique individual, driven by a vision, a sense of purpose and an understanding of the technology he would help create. Second, Facebook had some powerful financial backing, from Peter Thiel, Microsoft, and others. Perhaps most important of all, these sources of funding allowed

WORDS TO UNDERSTAND

acquisition strategy   the plan by which a company buys, or acquires, other companies or products

algorithm a process designed for a computer to follow to accomplish a certain task

caching placing information in a temporary storage area in a computer

hyper-partisan   believing far too strongly in only one point of view or only one side of an argument

irrelevant   having nothing to do with the subject at hand

piecemeal put together in haphazard fashion

relevant   well connected to the subject at hand

Facebook to hire teams of the best and brightest engineers in the world, all collaborating on a shared vision.

Facebook's game-changing tech lies in four main areas:

1. Indexing
2. Coding and computing technologies
3. Mobile technologies
4. Acquisitions

Let's take a look at each of these to see how they've helped Facebook evolve.

Indexing

What is indexing? Indexing is a fancy word for "searching." And that's what Facebook's algorithm does, constantly. Every time you open Facebook, every time you or your friends make a post, every time you do anything on Facebook, the indexing **algorithm** adds it to your internal profile. Why? To make the user experience tailored to your wants and needs.

The Facebook ranking algorithm assigns a value to everything in an effort to bring the information most **relevant** to you personally into your feed. Like any high-level artificial intelligence, the Facebook algorithm learns so that it can get better. It learns every time you like or dislike one of the news items it places in your feed, and it learns anytime you search for something new.

Of course, like any computer program, the Facebook index-ing process ultimately relies on the human engineers behind it. As smart as the algorithm may seem, it can only do what it is told by its programmers. As the old saying goes, "garbage in, garbage out." That means if Facebook's programmers get it wrong, you can end up with **irrelevant** or useless data in your feed. But this is part of the reason why Facebook has succeeded while earlier competitors fell short—Mark Zuckerberg and his team funda-mentally understand how to improve the user experience. Part of

The keys to Facebook are the ever-changing algorithms that drive it.

Is Facebook Dangerous?

Facebook is an undeniable success story, as evidenced by its ever-growing user numbers. However, is it possible that something so popular could actually be dangerous?

According to social psychologist Dr. Adam Alter, social media as a whole might actually be addictive, which can harm real-life relationships. As quoted in *The New York Times*, Dr. Alter states that, "Today, we're checking our social media constantly, which disrupts work and everyday life. We've become obsessed with how many 'likes' our Instagram photos are getting instead of where we are walking and whom we are talking to."

A study conducted by researchers at MIT and Harvard unearthed

a bigger problem with Facebook. According to the researchers' analysis of more than 1.25 million stories published during the 2016 presidential election cycle, social media was used ". . . as a backbone to transmit a **hyper-partisan** perspective to the world," resulting in the spread of "fake news" that became a symbol of the election.

Another area of concern is the access that Facebook gives outsiders to your own personal information. While you can tailor your privacy settings on the site to restrict what others can see, not all users either know or use these settings. The result is that a lot of personal information can be found by people with nefarious purposes. For example, if you share that you are going to be on vacation for two weeks and post that on Facebook so that the whole world can see it, you are opening yourself up to the potential that someone could use that information for criminal purposes. Younger Facebook users in particular should be aware of the danger that online stalkers could be reading their Facebook posts to potentially harm or take advantage of them.

Ultimately, you should take the same precautions with Facebook that you should with any other online site or tool. Understand that not everything you read on the Internet, even from Facebook, is true; take precautions to protect your private information; and practice everything in moderation.

the reason the Facebook experience seems flawless on the surface is due to the advanced technology "under the hood."

Coding and Computing Technologies

Facebook uses some pretty advanced coding and computing to serve its massive user base. Here's a quick sample of some of the hi-tech behind Facebook:

Haystack—Facebook's video storage and retrieval system. Facebook serves more than 1.2 million photos *per second*; this kind of data overload requires some advanced photo software to process, categorize, and maintain.

Bigpipe—to facilitate the faster loading of pages, Facebook relies on a web page serving system that sends over information in a **piecemeal** fashion; for example, your news feed is retrieved separately from the ads that appear on your pages in order to make everything fall into place rapidly.

Memcached—a memory **caching** system that has been optimized by Facebook for rapid retrieval of data.

HipHop for PHP—rather than the style of music, HipHop for PHP converts the scripting language PHP

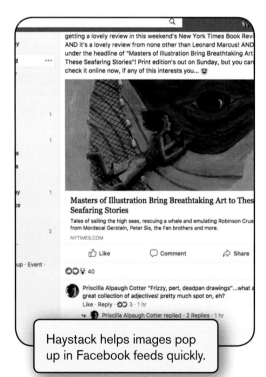

Haystack helps images pop up in Facebook feeds quickly.

Software working overtime results in the familiar Facebook welcome screen.

into C++ code, which results in faster performance on the site. This was developed in-house at Facebook and took 18 months to create.

Varnish—a program that makes photos and profile pictures appear at lightning fast speed.

While most of these are advanced coding applications, there's a simple idea behind them all: to serve up as much content as possible to the people who need it as rapidly as possible.

Mobile Technologies

Perhaps more than any other company, Facebook has bene-
fited from a shift in the way that consumers use the internet. Early on, Mark Zuckerberg understood that users were going
to use their smartphones to access the internet more and more,
as society became more mobile-oriented. Mark helped position
Facebook to get the benefits.

As recently as late 2012, Facebook's mobile revenue was
zero. Not a single dollar was earned from mobile technologies. By

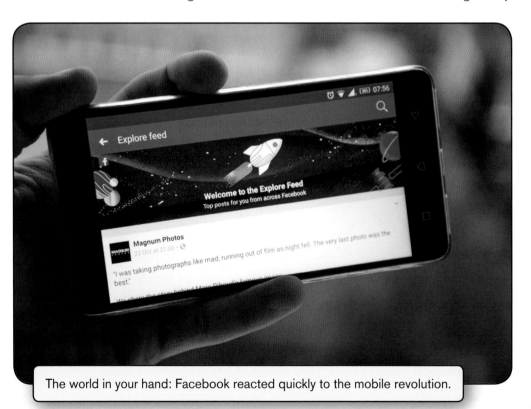

The world in your hand: Facebook reacted quickly to the mobile revolution.

Inside Facebook technology

2017, Facebook's mobile revenue represented an amazing 84 percent of the company's total ad revenue, at $7.2 billion. Year over year, Facebook's mobile revenue growth rate was 80 percent.

Just as in 2012, Mark again sees a huge opportunity in mobile technologies—this time, with mobile video. "I've said before that I see video as a megatrend on the same order as mobile," Zuckerberg said in late 2016. "That's why we're going to keep putting video first across our family of apps and making it easier for people to capture and share video in new ways."

The Facebook Live feature allows users to broadcast a live video feed to their friends or even to the general public while on Facebook. The company also introduced a Video tab on its Facebook app and even indicated an intention to develop original content. As Mark said, "We're looking for ways to grow the eco-system of video content on Facebook. We want people to think of Facebook as a place for interesting and relevant video content from professional creators as well as their friends."

Being at the leading edge of the next wave of mobile technologies is likely to help Facebook continue its upward growth.

Acquisitions

While Facebook has grown just fine on its own, part of what has helped its explosive growth is its **acquisition strategy**.

Facebook used its success to grow, partly by acquiring other apps.

Facebook has already acquired more than 50 companies, most notably messenger service WhatsApp for a whopping $19 billion.

Acquisitions help Facebook grow faster in many ways, but they're all linked to information. For example, with the WhatsApp deal, Facebook got access to a user base that it may not have had information on before. This let it expand the reach of its indexing algorithm. As writer David Meyer explained in *Fortune* magazine: "Let's say someone named Peter has decided to remain private [by declining to tell Facebook his phone number or the email address he shares with other people]. Jane, who knows Peter and has his contact details, joins Facebook and uploads her address book. But Facebook can't suggest Peter as a friend because it doesn't have the same details about him. With the two systems being linked, if Peter uses WhatsApp, then Facebook will now be able to suggest him as a friend to Jane."

WhatsApp also brings a new user base to Facebook to allow it to do what it does best—index information so that it can provide relevant ads to users. The more relevant ads that Facebook

WhatsApp is especially popular outside the United States.

Facebook's purchase of Instagram added a great deal to the company's profit.

provides to more people, the more money it can make from ad revenue.

Facebook's other most noteworthy acquisition was when it purchased Instagram for $1 billion in 2012. Instagram is an immensely popular photo-sharing application that is known for its stylized photo technology. As of September 2017, Instagram boasted 800 million users, including 500 million active daily users. Of particular note to Facebook's revenue stream, Instagram also reported a doubling of advertisers on the platform—up to 2 million—from March to September 2017. While Instagram's $1 billion price may have seemed like a lot in 2012, Facebook proved savvy with this purchase, as analysts now peg Instagram's value at between $25 and $50 billion.

Text-Dependent Questions

1. What are the ways in which Facebook can be considered dangerous?

2. What role has mobile played in Facebook's growth?

3. Name two of Facebook's most significant acquisitions?

Research Project

One of the concerns that has dogged Facebook since its was founded is the issue of privacy. Research the privacy settings that Facebook offers and find out which data you post on the site can truly be considered private. Are some settings more private than others? How can you be even more secure when using a social network like Facebook?

4

Now and the Future

Mark Zuckerberg has become famous for the success he's had with Facebook. But he's not done yet. Mark and Facebook have big plans for the future, in the worlds of virtual reality, artificial intelligence, and more. Through a combination of **humanitarian** and business-driven efforts, he's still looking to make an even bigger mark on the world. For example, Mark has personally signed the Giving Pledge, an agreement among some of the world's wealthiest people to give away at least half of their money to charity over time. However, he and his company are also facing some serious challenges, especially regarding how it uses the private information of its users.

One of Mark's primary global plans is to change the world by getting every single person on the Earth connected to the Internet. To achieve that goal, he's started Internet.org. In 2013, he told *Wired* magazine:

WORDS TO UNDERSTAND

humanitarian focusing on helping other people

moral imperative something that a person strongly believes that they feel they must act on simply because it is the right thing to do

"Over the past few years, we've invested more than a billion dollars in connecting people in developing countries. We have a product called Facebook for Every Phone, which provides our service on feature phones; it has 100 million users. But no one company or government can build out a full stack of infrastructure to support this around the world. So you need to work together with folks. Since we've announced Internet.org, we've heard from operators around the world and governments who want to work with us. This is going to provide momentum to make this work over the next three to five years, or however long it's going to take."

One of the ways Facebook is achieving Mark's vision is the Alliance for Affordable Internet, a program Facebook began along with partners such as Google and Ericsson. The Alliance works towards cheaper Internet access by changing government rules. While the company would obviously benefit financially from more people getting on the Internet and using Facebook, Mark also sees these efforts as a moral imperative to get afford-able Internet access to the whole world. It may be hard to grasp this, but the fact remains that fewer than 3 billion of the world's 7 billion people actually have access to the internet.

To that end, Facebook has also introduced a project, known as Terragraph, that hopes to transform the way the internet works.

Terragraph

The Terragraph project uses wireless technology to bring super-fast internet to urban areas, without the problems of laying fiber optic cable. The early plans for this new wireless network have speeds of more than one gigabyte per second, which is

Look for more of these ARIES antennas as part of the Terragraph rollout.

just as fast as the wired connections offered by Google Fiber and about 100 times the speed of the average U.S. wired connection. Terragraph is powered by a wireless technology known as WiGig. Facebook is betting that this is the right technology to use, as WiGig is already slated for use in future gadgets from companies like Samsung, Qualcomm, and Intel. While challenges exist, Facebook believes that this is the wave of the future. The company intends to give away the designs behind the technology for free, hoping that telecommunications providers adopt it.

Spaces

When Facebook acquired virtual reality company Oculus in 2014 for $2 billion, no one was really sure where Facebook was headed. The roadmap for Facebook's vision began to roll out in 2017, with the introduction of Spaces. Spaces is Facebook's first attempt to bring its social network to the realm of virtual reality.

Using the Oculus Rift VR device, Spaces is a digital world that you can inhabit with up three users simultaneously. The idea is that you can use a digital projection of yourself to "hang out" virtually with some of your friends, who are also digitally projected into the system. Ultimately, the platform is designed to allow you to play games and interact more directly with other participants who are also on the Oculus Rift system.

In its early phase, Spaces can use Facebook Messenger video, even if users do not have an Oculus Rift. Ultimately, the company wants to add AR (augmented reality), in which apps allow you to overlay "reality" with various filters to create an enhanced—or "augmented"—experience.

While the success of these platforms is not guaranteed, it's rarely been a smart move to bet against Mark Zuckerberg and Facebook in the past. Just like his vision of a social network seemed revolutionary at the time, a world in which everyone is connected on the Internet and has access to virtual and augmented reality may seem futuristic, too. However, the once-revolutionary idea of a social network is now a part of daily life, and these innovations may one day be the same.

Check out the Oculus VR system

Privacy Concerns

In 2018, it was revealed that a company called Cambridge Analytica had used information obtained from 87 million Facebook users to lobby for the campaign of President Trump. Many Facebook users were very upset that their information had been sold this way. Facebook, under pressure, said that the information had been gleaned from users via an online quiz and that Cambridge had then bought that information. According to Facebook's own policies, this was an unauthorized use of their data. The company put out a public apology via newspaper and online ads. Zuckerberg was called before Congress to answer questions about the data breach.

In the weeks after the scandal hit, the price of Facebook stock plunged, falling at one point to 17 percent from its previous high mark. The investigation into the issue was ongoing at press time. The Federal Trade Commission is looking into how it happened and how Facebook might be punished. European authorities were also looking at ways to limit the exposure of its residents to data mining like this.

Overall, the incident made very clear one of the downsides of the app and many others like it that gather personal information from users. That downside is the danger of that information being used in the wrong way, either for over-aggressive lobbying, the creation of "fake news," or the targeting of particular groups.

Having an app and a site that connects so many millions of

people can have many positive benefits. But it's still a relative-ly new process and there are hidden dangers and problems that need to be dealt with. Facebook is not alone in not handling the data is takes care of well, but its worldwide popularity probably means that it's here to stay as it battles through those problems.

Text-Dependent Questions

1. Explain how Terragraph works. Why is it so useful?

2. What are VR and AR, and what role do they play in Facebook's road map?

3. What is Internet.org, and how does it seek to change the world?

Research Project

This chapter indicates that Mark Zuckerberg is working to give back some of his fortune to the world, helping others who are in need. Using the Internet, find out some of the charities that Mark supports. How much money has he given away? How does he use his personal time to help others? What goals does he have for improving the world?

FIND OUT MORE

Books:

Gilbert, Sara. **Built for Success: The Story of Facebook.** Mankato, MN: Creative Paperbacks, 2013.

Hoefflinger, Mike. **Becoming Facebook: The 10 Challenges That Defined the Company That's Disrupting the World.** New York: AMACOM, 2017.

Kirkpatrick, David. **The Facebook Effect: The Inside Story of the Company That Is Connecting the World.** New York: Simon & Schuster, 2011.

Mezrich, Ben. **The Accidental Billionaires: The Founding of Facebook: A Tale of Sex, Money, Genius and Betrayal.** New York: Doubleday, 2009.

On the Internet:

Mark Zuckerberg's page on Facebook
www.facebook.com/Zuck

Mashable: Mark Zuckerberg
mashable.com/category/mark-zuckerberg

Facebook Fast Fact: CNN Library
http://www.cnn.com/2014/02/11/world/facebook-fast-facts/index.html

SERIES GLOSSARY OF KEY TERMS

algorithm a process designed for a computer to follow to accomplish a certain task

colleagues the people you work with.

entrepreneurs people who start their own businesses, often taking financial risks to do so.

incorporate sold shares of stock to become a publicly traded company

innovation creativity, the process of building something new

open-source describing a computer program that can be used by any programmer to create or modify the product

perks benefits to doing something.

startups new companies just starting out.

targeting trying to reach a certain person or thing.

venture capitalists people who invest money in young companies in hopes they will grow greatly in value

Tech 2.0

INDEX

Photo Credits

Alamy Stock Photo: RGR Collection 40. ARIES: 57. Dreamstime.com: Dolphfyn 6; Peterfactors 10; Jannis Werner 21; Featureflash 22; Editor27 26; Maksym Protsenko 31; David Molina 32; Peter Ksinan 34, 48; Schyther5 35; Maciek905 43; Ocusfocus 44; Sdecoret 45; Sunju1004 47; Dennizn 50; Ldprod 51; GilbertC 52; Kavastudio 59. Luc Van Braekel/Flickr: 24. Dustin Moskovitz/Wikimedia/CC: 20. Newscom: David Silpa/UPI 16; Karen T. Borchers/MCT 26; Terry Schmitt/UPI 36. Shutterstock: catwalker 9, 54; MidoSemSem 30; Frederic LeGrand/Comeo 35; Andrey Popov 47. Wikimedia: Pointsofnoreturn 12, transmarinus 15; World Economic Forum/Andy Mettler: 28.

About the Author

John Csiszar is a freelance writer and article curator. After graduating from UCLA, Csiszar was a registered investment advisor for 19 years before becoming a writer and editor. In addition to writing thousands of articles for online publications, including The Huffington Post, he has created, edited, and curated a variety of technology-oriented projects, from web pages and social media text to software help manuals. Csiszar lives in Hermosa Beach, California.